# Banaban Cultural Identity

Raobeia Ken Sigrah
Stacey M. King

BANABAN VISION PUBLICATIONS

Gold Coast, Australia

Banaban Cultural Identity
Copyright © Raobeia Ken Sigrah and Stacey M. King.
All rights reserved.
Published by Banaban Vision Publications
PO Box 1116 Paradise Point. Qld. 4216. Australia
www.banabanvision.com

 A catalogue record for this work is available from the National Library of Australia

ISBNs: Paperback: 978-0-6451491-6-6
Ebook: 978-0-6451491-8-0

This book may not be reproduced in any form or by any electronic or mechanical means, including information storage and retrieval system, without permission in writing from the authors. The only exception is a reviewer who may quote short excerpts in a review.

Cover designed by Stacey King

This content was written by the authors and presented at:
ISLANDS of the WORLD VIII International Conference
"Changing Islands – Changing Worlds"
1-7 November 2004, Kinmen Island (Quemoy), Taiwan

The authors have provided information sourced from original documents, photographs, and interviews, which are either owned or kindly donated to the authors. All other reference material has been sourced as quoted. Internal diagrams were created and/or supplied by the authors.

# DEDICATION

## Raobeia Ken Sigrah
1956-2021
Banaban Clan spokesman and historian

Your name will live on in history as a true Banaban warrior and a proud descendant of his people, who gave your people the greatest gift:

*"Hold your head high and be forever proud of being BANABAN and ensure Banaban identity is never lost but passed on to future generations".*

*"Our ancestors passed on their strength, resilience, and determination through traditional knowledge. We owe it to them to listen."*

Raobeia Ken Sigrah.


*"Banaban culture has endured centuries of adversity and upheaval. Today, assimilation poses the most significant threat to Banaban identity."*

Stacey M. King

# Contents

Introduction ............................................................. 3
1. Indigenous Banabans ........................................... 5
2. Early Invasions Before European Discovery ...... 11
3. European Contact ............................................... 17
4. European Recording of Banaban History ......... 23
5. The Alienation of Banaban Identity by Colonial Historians and Academics ..................................... 29
6. The Use of Language to Define Ethnic Identity and Influence of Missionaries ................................ 35
7. Definition of Banaban Identity and the Value of Land ........................................................................ 39
8. Te Aka Discovery ................................................ 43
9. Banaban assimilation – fact or fiction .............. 51
10. Banabans Today Living Under Two Governments – Fiji and Kiribati ............................ 55
11. Conclusion ........................................................ 61
References ............................................................. 63
About the Authors ................................................ 67
Other Titles By The Authors ................................ 73

# Photographs

1. Pacific Map showing locations Banaba and Rabi, Fiji. ...................................................................1
2. Banabans gathering for batere (dance performances) early 1900s (Postcard). ............................ 2
3. Banaban preparing for dance performance early 1900s ...............................................................4
4. Banaban dances wearing Te Aka wigs during a te karanga dance performance prior 1910. ............. 7
5. BANABA (Ocean Island) prior to 1500, before ..10
6. BANABAN (Ocean Island) 1500 onwards after the ........................................................................13
7. Auriaria and Nei Anginimaeao would arrive on Banaba in te waa , ocean going outriggers (Miller Collection (1907-1939). ...........................................15
8. BANABA (Ocean Island) 1600 onwards after the ............................................................................. 16
9. Original copy Gilbert Islands Proclamation dated 1892.................................................................21
10. Albert Ellis, first camp when he arrived on Banaba....................................................................... 22
11. Harry Maude, Native Lands Commissioner Banaba 1930s (Maude Collection). ........................... 27
12. A young Arthur Grimble in his office as Resident Commissioner c. 1920 (Williams Collection 1902-31). ............................................................... 28

13. Early Christian converts on Banaba led by a Missionary Pastor called Solomon (Ellis 1900).... 33

14. The new Banaban tani Kiritian (Christian) congregation on Banaba early 1900s (Broadbent Collection)...............34

15. Banaban words from Maude's Notebook 1932...38

16. Cultural Law, Te Rii ni Banaba: Know your genealogy, inherited family role, and name of your hamlet. ...............41

17, Phosphate mining nearing Te Aka village site in 1965...............42

18. Archeological dig conducted at the old Te Aka village site...............50

19. First Banaban generation born on Rabi, Fiji after 1945...............54

20. Banaban Elders on Rabi, 1995 (S. King Collection). ............... 56

21. The authors returning the female remains recovered from the Te Aka dig by Lampert in 1960s to the Te Aka Clan residing on Rabi Island, 2000. ............... 66

22. The authors meeting with Dr Lampert at ANU, Canberra 1997 to arrange the return of artefacts recovered from Te Aka dig in 1960s. (S. King Collection 1997). ...............72

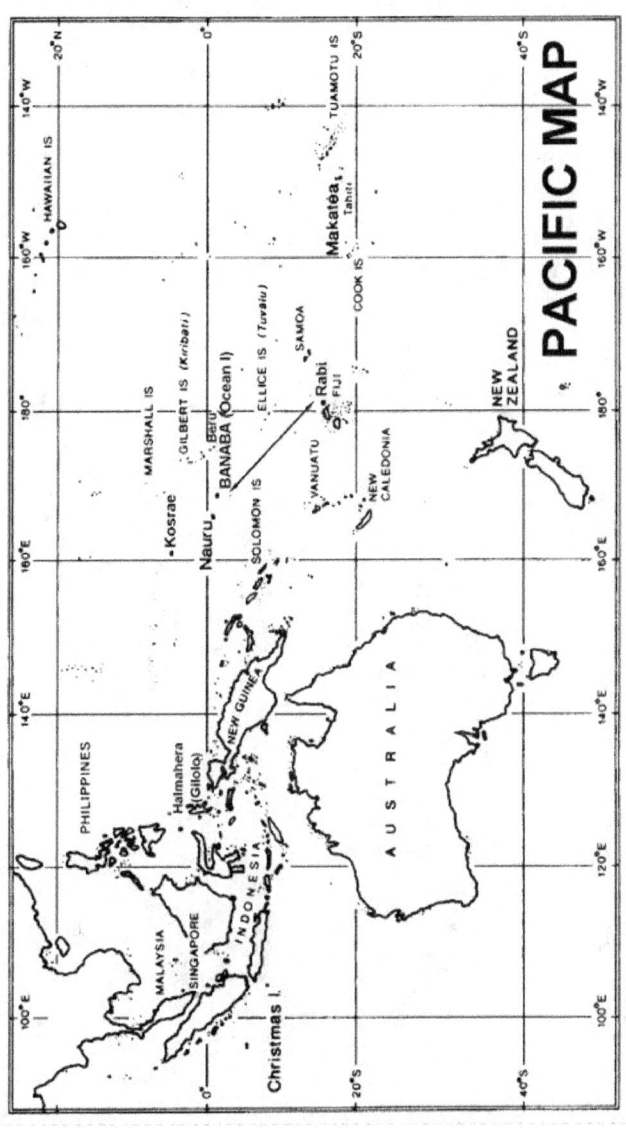

1. Pacific Map showing locations Banaba and Rabi, Fiji.

2. Banabans gathering for *batere* (dance performances) early 1900s (Postcard).

# Introduction

The question regarding the cultural identity of Banabans has become contentious, opening a 'Pandora's Box' of associated issues. With the discovery of phosphate on Banaba in 1900 and the subsequent arrival of a British-owned mining company, the indigenous inhabitants would be manipulated, and their island totally overrun by the Company's operations.

Leading up to World War Two, there was no doubts or questions over Banaban identity. By examining the historical processes that led to what many perceive as the assimilation of the Banaban people with the I-Kiribati, their Pacific Island neighbours, and the endeavours undertaken to try and obliterate Banaban identity altogether.

This study analyses the facts and identifies what is fiction and the role certain historical events played in aiding the formation of the current status quo of the Banaban people socially and politically today.

The issue of Banaban cultural identity and its complexities also highlights the strength of a culture that for many years has withstood the full gamut of adversities, which in most cases were intentionally used to repress the Banabans.

Claims that the Banabans are now I-Kiribati, mainly through intermarriage and the loss of the Banaban language, is an assumption made by others and one that belies the Banaban claim for survival as an original Oceanic people.

3. Banaban preparing for dance performance early 1900s (A. Ellis Collection).

# 1. Indigenous Banabans

The indigenous inhabitants of Banaba are recognised by the Banaban people today as the secretive and shy Te Aka people. The word Te Aka means 'the first hamlet', a small group of dwellings inhabited by members of the same family (Sigrah & King 2001:26).

The following key features of Te Aka were documented by Sigrah and King:

- distinct in appearance and physical stature
- their worship of the fire or sun as their totem
- myths and legends that support the authenticity of their ethnic identity
- land division on Banaba supports their land ownership
- Known site of the sacred cairns on the island and Te Aka clan traditions also endorse the orthodox European view of the settlement of Banaba.

Another description of the Te Aka stated, 'they are described as being small-bodied, squat, crinkly haired, large-eared and black-skinned and were skilful in sorcery' (Maude & Maude 1932:263).

Sigrah and King (2001) have documented further evidence of a distinct Te Aka appearance:

> Te Aka ancestors had long jaws, seen in many skulls well preserved in sacred family bangota (ancestral shrines) right up until the time that Banabans were forcibly removed from the island during the Japanese occupation in World War II.

Maude and Lampert also noted this evidence:

> They are apparently burial mounds, and at one situated under a mango tree near the site of the former maneaba in the hamlet called Te Aka, one could see the skulls of both the long-jawed and the short-jawed people through gaps between the stones: at least as late as 1903 (Maude 1995:106).

> ... the skulls referred to are under a low stone cairn and could be seen through gaps between the stones. They were skulls of both 'the long-jawed and short-jawed people'. The cairn was named Te Burita, which has the meaning ... 'an enchanted place, dangerous to visit' (Bingham 1908:79) and was situated under a mango tree near the *maneaba* at Te Aka. It was said to be still extant as late as 1964, apparently until the ground surface beneath the tree

was bulldozed flat so that workmen's huts could be erected in the shade (Lampert 1965:3).

The Te Aka recognise the place of Te Burita cairn as the second known sacred site where two large *teitai* (*Calophyllum inopohyllum*) trees grew. In Te Aka legends, they are known as the 'ship trees'. The Te Aka had names for these two significant trees, 'one called te Burita, which is also the name of their war canoe, and the other tree called Te Itimoa, meaning first lightning' (Sigrah & King 2001: 29).

4. Banaban dances wearing Te Aka wigs during a *te karanga* dance performance prior 1910.

The Te Aka were known for their skills and powerful sorcery, 'a power they possessed from the worship of their ancestral skulls' (Ellis 1936; Grimble 1921; Lampert 1968).

What is apparent from Banaban legends is that Te Aka were land dwellers and had no concept of seafaring. The island's surrounding fringing reefs supplied them with all their needs. Another endorsement of Te Aka's distinct appearance is the presence of 'thick, black crinkly hair' that was so prized that even until modern times, Te Aka descendants made wigs from the hair of their deceased ancestors and wore these wigs on special ceremonial occasions. Photographic evidence supporting this was published by Sigrah and King (2001:28; 160).

Te Aka has other features, such as language, certain games, the sport of boxing, and a unique dance that has withstood the passing of time.

*Te karanga,* or stick dance, is a war-chant style dance offering insight into the old Te Aka ways. It provides a snippet of the lost Banaban dialect in the chants that, unfortunately, have virtually been lost, and only a few words remain today (Photo 6).

The first recorded account of *te karanga* dance was in 1896 and published in 1908 by British Colonial Offical Arthur Mahaffy. He offered a detailed report of what he deemed 'one very curious and beautiful dance, which I have never seen elsewhere'.

He went on to describe the dance in detail:

> The performers are drawn up in two lines facing each other, and each dancer is equipped with a staff about six feet long, decorated with feathers and coloured streamers. A long recitative is sung by the leader, at the completion of which the two lines of dancers engage in a most complicated set of figures, passing in and out through the spaces between the performers with wonderful precision. As each man passes his neighbour, he raises his staff above his head and clashes it against the next one in absolute unison. The effect is very fine, and figure follows figure in great variety, always preceded by the chanting of a recitative. The dress of the dancers is also peculiar: they were upon their heads conical caps woven on coconut leaves, and from their waists, almost to the ground, hang petticoats made of the same leaf.

The Banabans have recorded genealogies of Te Aka with Sigrah and King (2001:59), stating that Sigrah's own Te Aka family lineage had been documented back to at least the 1500s. He also believed that their Godfather and head of their clan, Teimanaia, could go back well beyond this period.

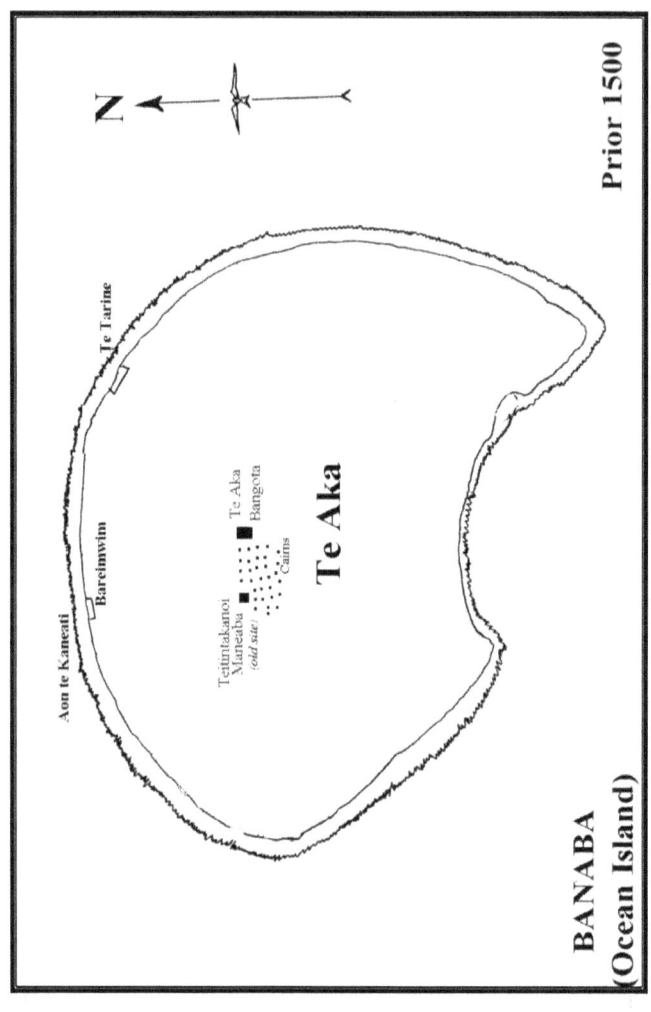

5. BANABA (Ocean Island) prior to 1500, before known Invasions.

# 2. Early Invasions Before European Discovery

In Banaban history, we know of two recorded invasions before European discovery in the early 1800s. The first was Auriaria and his party in the late 14th century from Gilolo in the East Indies, now known as Halmahera, Indonesia. This invasion signified that 'they came as warriors...' (Sigrah & King 2001:91) denotes the subsequent conflict and warfare that ensued during this period of Banaban history.

After various battles, the island was divided into two separate divisions, the northern portion of which they named Te Aononanne. Located from the densely forested highlands surrounding the various Te Aka hamlets and the nearby *bangota* sacred cairns down to the northern coastline and fringing reefs. These battles are believed to be responsible for the creation of *te karanga* dance. Another specific dance that developed during this period was *te karanga are e uarereke* (the short stick dance), which is a re-enactment of the land disputes that began after Auriaria's arrival. These new arrivals would be known for their skills in seafaring and as warriors.

Because of Te Aka's reputation as skilled sorcerers, they were respected and feared, creating a veil of silence and secrecy surrounding them. Even the name Te Aonnoanne, meaning 'that place!', endorses this belief in the power of Te Aka's sorcery. To utter the word 'Te Aka' could bring about a curse.

Auriaria and his descendants soon learned to respect the Te Aka, preferring to keep their distance. They would eventually become known as the Auriaria clan, inhabiting and settling on the island's southwest region, which became known by the old Banaban word 'Tabwewa', meaning 'to the south'. (Photo: 6).

The second invasion of Banaba in the later part of the 15th century is quoted by Sigrah and King as '… they came in peace' (2001:117). This aptly describes the arrival of a group of islanders headed by a woman called Nei Anginimaeao from a southern Gilbert Island called Beru.

According to Arthur Grimble's *Tungaru Traditions* (1989), her arrival relates to the Battles of Kaitu and Uakeia, when the two chiefs of Beru fought and conquered nearly every island in Kiribati in about 1680.

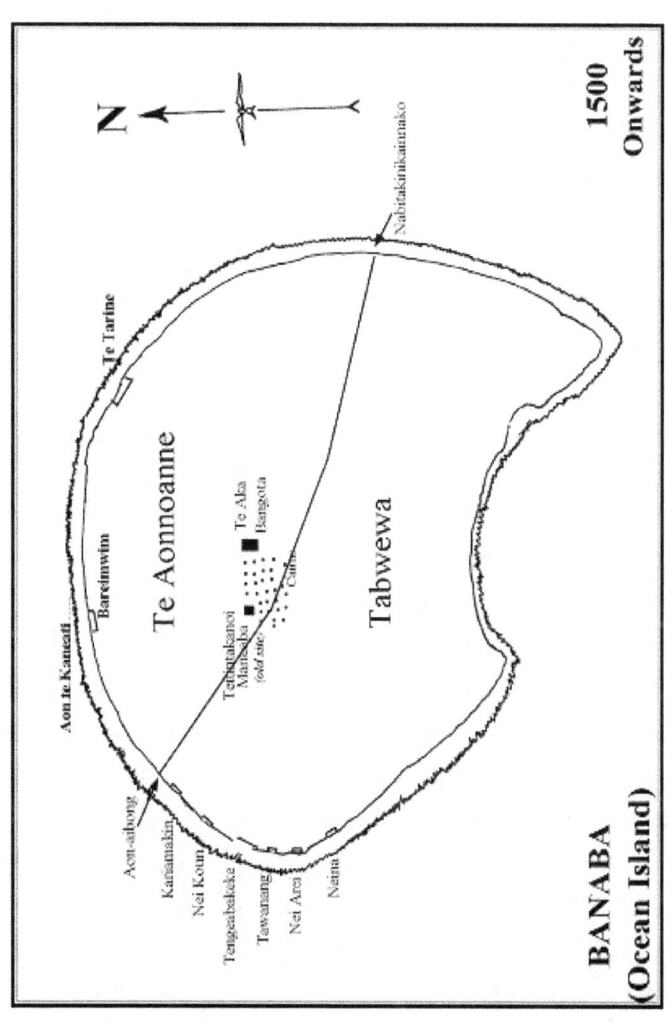

6. BANABAN (Ocean Island) 1500 onwards after the First Invasion.

Nei Anginimaeao's arrival would coincide with her group fleeing these upheavals in search of new land or becoming driftaways.

Unlike the first, this group was invited by the Banabans living in the Tabwewa region to stay and settle on Banaba.

Once again, new divisions were made within this southern area, while the Te Aka upheld their original land boundaries in the region of Te Aononanne.

This invasion also brings the first interaction and influence of Gilbertese (I-Kiribati) culture. What is also significant about this period is that the indigenous Banabans, the Te Aka, were still reluctant to interact with these new arrivals even with the inter-marriage of Nei Anginimaeao's brother, Na Kouteba into the Te Aka clan.

Clear land boundaries were still observed. However, new rituals and customs associated with Gilbertese traditions were introduced, and these new land divisions covered the areas surrounding the island's only suitable landing place (Photo 6).

This important aspect also gave these newcomers more contact with ships calling on this more protected side of the island, where certain family clans from the original Tabwewa descendants upheld the right to board foreign vessels, a custom the Tabwewans had created even before the arrival of Nei Anginimaeao.

What is acknowledged by the Banabans is that until the arrival of the missionaries and mining industry on Banaba, 'the indigenous Te Aka, the sorcerers, were the nucleus of Banaban society. Auriaria, the warriors, and Nei Anginimaeao, who came in peace, strengthened the foundations of our civilisation' (Sigrah & King 2001: 166).

This rich collection of oral traditions has been passed down by Banaban forefathers for centuries. It has withstood not only the influence of time but also insurmountable upheavals, and yet, it has survived.

7. Auriaria and Nei Anginimaeao would arrive on Banaba in *te waa*, ocean going outriggers (Miller Collection (1907-1939).

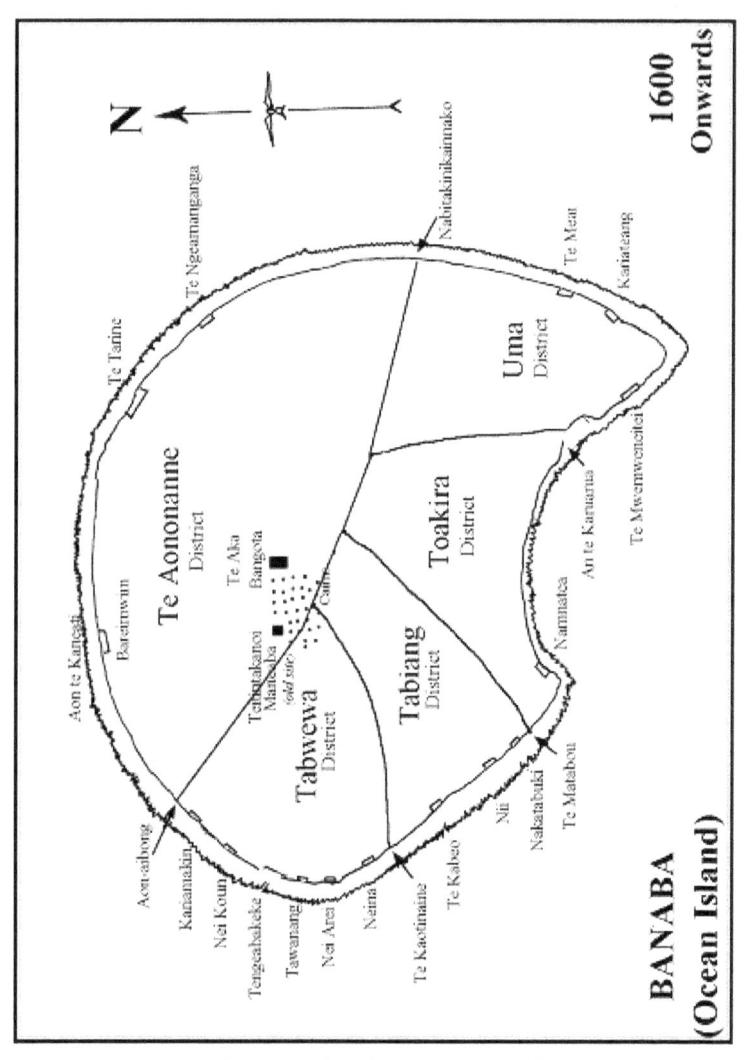

8. BANABA (Ocean Island) 1600 onwards after the second invasion.

# 3. European Contact

The first recorded mention of Banaba—also known as Paanopa or Panapa, based on the island's indigenous pronunciation—appears in whaling journals and diaries from the early 1800s onward. During this period, ships would stop at the island 'to buy meat (pigs) and to add fresh food to their sea rations while on their year-long journeys' (Mahaffy 1910:569).

Paanopa would become known by European seamen as Ocean Island after the discovery of the island by Captain John Mertho in 1804 and named after his ship Ocean.

For the next century, Banabans would begin to come into more contact with the outside world as whaling ships discovered what they referred to as 'on-the-line grounds', which extended along the waters of the equator from the Line Island in the east to Nauru in the west (Sigrah & King 2001:177).

During this period, the Banabans also came into contact with runaway convicts who had jumped ship while on their way to penal settlements in New

South Wales or Norfolk Island. By 1985, records show that 17 convicts had settled on Banaba under what would commonly become known throughout the Pacific as 'beachcombers'.

Mahaffy stated, 'they were usually bad, adopted the dress of the natives, and were tattooed like them; instructed them in all the vices of a 'superior' civilisation, and communicated to them its most terrible diseases'. He also mentions that a well-respected sea captain who visited Ocean Island in 1852 on a whaling ship had related that, 'in their general character, the white beachcombers of that place were no better than those on Pleasant Island'.

What Mahaffy has recorded is the impact these beachcombers had on the local Banaban community in his 1910 article:

> They taught them to distil a spirit from cocoa-nut-toddy through gun-barrels; they mended the dilapidated muskets which the natives possessed; they practised polygamy; they brawled among themselves, and not infrequently murdered and poisoned each other... Wars were of frequent occurrence among the natives of the four villages on the island, and in these struggles, the white men took a leading part and were sometimes killed. (Mahaffy 1910:580)

Mahaffy concluded that he found no lasting memory of the beachcombers among the Banabans other than that 'they were bad men', and they left 'no abiding mark' on the Banaban society by his first visit to the island in 1896.

The other significant influence during this pre-phosphate period, as Banabans began to interact more with European ship crews, was recruiting young Banaban men to join their crews and later find themselves labourers on foreign plantations. This phenomenon would become known throughout the Pacific as 'blackbirding'.

If the entry recorded in the diary of Captain Mackay aboard the Queensland brig Flora in 1875 is any indication when he stated that, 'after they recruited 60 Banaban men to take to Queensland, he was approached by the elder from Tabwewa who with tears in his eyes, the elder said that most of their men had already been taken away...' (Sigrah & King 2001:177), then large numbers of young Banaban men were taken from their homeland.

With these major influences of European contact over this period, we find documented census figures gathered over a hundred years from 1851 to 1945 and published by Sigrah and King (2001:184-185).

The data gathered states a Banaban population in 1851 of '2,000-3,000' (Webster 1851; Maude 1994:77), and by 4th August 1885, a massive population drop to '200 or more' (Walkup 1885; Maude 1994:90).

By the arrival of Ellis on 11 May 1900 and the discovery of phosphate on Banaba, his diary records a total of 451 Banabans. Ellis and other Pacific historians, Arthur Grimble and Harry Maude, would contribute to a prolonged drought experienced on the island between 1871 and 1874.

Walkup and Maude would also claim reports of the population on Banaba falling 'to between a dozen and 40 people'. Sigrah and King argue that 'if so few Banabans had survived, the genealogical charts would reflect these losses with the disappearance of whole family lines. Sigrah's charts show some losses but not to this extent' (2001:186).

Ellis used this fact to his advantage and promised the local community that the presence of his mining operations would also be able to provide them with water. The Banabans did not realise
they would also have to pay for this privilege.

Not much was known or had been written about the origins of Banabas' indigenous inhabitants leading up to the discovery of phosphate by Albert Ellis in 1900. As Mahaffy (1910:570) stated, 'the men were a fine athletic race, wonderfully clever in managing their outrigger canoes, and rather dark in colour when compared with the Gilbert Islanders, the result of their constant exposure to the equatorial sun'. He also concluded that, 'it is because I have never seen any record of their older state that I have endeavoured to collect in these notes some of the impressions of a six months stay among them.'

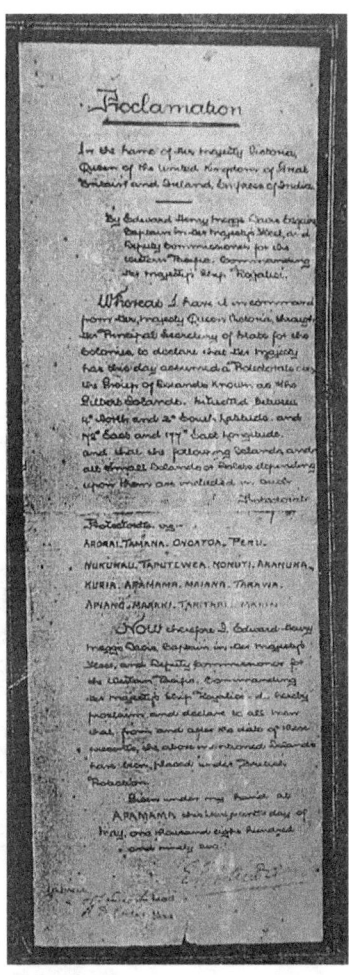

9. Original copy Gilbert Islands Proclamation dated 1892.
Banaba (Paanopa) was not included.

10. Albert Ellis, first camp when he arrived on Banaba (Ocean Island) 1900.

# 4. European Recording of Banaban History

By the time of Ellis' discovery of phosphate, Banaba was a remote and isolated community. Even at the time of Great Britain's Protectorate over what would become known as the Gilbert Islands in 1892 (Photo 9), Banaba was not included in the Group, as stated by Maude 1975 in tabled evidence in the British court:

> Inter-locking world of the Gilbertese, Ocean Island and the Banabans, situated far to the west, had no part. Forgotten in Gilbertese tradition, unrecorded in the Gilbertese genealogies, it may be doubted if a single Gilbertese Islander was aware of the existence of the Banabans at the time of their first contact with Europeans. Ocean Island was no more part of the Gilbert Islands than Greenland was part of Norway a century or two after the Scandinavian

voyages had ceased. Like Nauru, it was a dead-end reached by occasional driftaways from the Gilbert Islands, but from which there was no return (Sigrah & King 2001:35).

It was during this period that misinterpretation of Banaban identity began.

The assumption that Banaba was controlled by chiefs was typical of Western thinking at the time. However, this was further exaggerated when Ellis had the Banaban man who came out to meet him on his arrival in 1900 place his mark of an agreement to mine the island for the next 999 years and declare him as the King of Ocean Island.

From the Banaban point of view, the negotiations would have seemed somewhat strange and mystifying. The proposal being made was absolutely new to them, and 'there was no way the Banabans could have foreseen its implications' (Williams & Macdonald 1985:31).

Ellis soon discovered that there were four different settlements. He termed them 'villages', in what is commonly referred to under the English concept of social organisation. In fact, this first assumption was another grave mistake as each settlement clearly represented the different clans and settlers living on the island who all upheld their own cultural practices and traditions (Photo 8).

In Banaban culture, all men and women are considered equal, and 'only elders within the community are elevated because of respect for their knowledge and understanding in all matters relating to culture and daily life' (Sigrah & King 2001:169).

Ellis would later state in his diary,

> 'It soon became evident that people in the other villages were aggrieved'. He discovered that the original two signatories on his agreement were trying to restrict trading to their own village. It was not until five days on the island that he realised that the land he wished to buy or lease was divided into innumerable private plots, and to acquire the areas needed to begin mining and shipping would involve reaching a separate agreement with almost every resident' (Williams & Macdonald 1985:34).

What Ellis did not understand or preferred to dismiss was the fact that each settlement consisted of *kainga* 'hamlets' with a central *maneaba* 'meeting house'. Banabans argue that villages were a new system introduced by the Europeans. Their people were brought together into one common land boundary with a central *maneaba* and church to assist the Company and government control the local inhabitants.

The Banabans believe 'the development of the village system brought about one of the most significant changes' (Sigrah & King 2001:218).

Ellis would soon learn that labouring for wages was not a local custom, and the idea of bringing in either Gilbertese or Caroline Islanders was raised as 'they had lived under British or German rule and had learned to work. The important thing was to be sure that the Ocean Island people understood that the Company must have the right to bring in foreigners' (Williams & Macdonald 1985:28).

In his 1910 article, Mahaffy also claims that when he had first visited Banaba in 1896, he had found it in the occupation 'of a purely native community' and even though the inhabitants were 'rather dark in colour when compared with the Gilbert Islanders ... they spoke the purest Gilbertine, and are beyond question members of that race: their tattooing closely resembled that of the Gilbert Islanders, with whom I was well acquainted'.

What is interesting is his assumption that because of the tattooing, he believed that this signified the entire population's Gilbertese lineage. In fact, tattooing is recognised amongst the Banabans as being introduced by the Tabwewans and is not recognised in Te Aka traditions (Sigrah & King 2001:164).

Later arrivals from the Gilberts living in the southern districts of Uma and Tabiang also used tattooing as one of their customs. Mahaffy would also confirm his observations by stating, 'I only landed for a short time at the village of Uma, on the south-east corner of the island'.

The mention of 'a pure Gilbertese language' is also interesting and suggests that it was not the typical language he had heard in his travels. Of course, what must be remembered during all these early European interactions is that observations were being made and viewed from a solely European perspective with no actual knowledge or understanding of the complexities of Banaban society.

11. Harry Maude, Native Lands Commissioner Banaba 1930s (Maude Collection).

12. A young Arthur Grimble in his office as Resident Commissioner c. 1920 (Williams Collection 1902-31).

# 5. The Alienation of Banaban Identity by Colonial Historians and Academics

As problems between the Banabans, the mining company and the Colonial government compounded, the re-writing of Banaban history started to evolve. The main catalyst was the interest in documenting the history of phosphate mining. But invariably the articles would reflect the lifestyle of the island's indigenous inhabitants as publishers and editors met the public's demand for stories regaling the exotic ways of this remote Pacific Isle.

Numerous books were published, and people such as Ellis, Grimble, Maude, Eliot, Mahaffy, and Pope, who had all started as Company or government staff, became best-selling authors. These publications had the power to shape and re-write history to suit the author's objectives, especially in the case of Ellis with him justifying the world benefits of his phosphate discovery.

Grimble's subsequent poetic style of writing became so popular that his books became part of the reading material in Australia's school curriculum at the time. While millions of Europeans enjoyed these men's vision of South Seas adventurers, the impact on the Banaban community would prove very detrimental.

It is important to remember that, in the period leading up to World War II, key figures like Resident Commissioner Arthur Grimble played a significant role in the major land disputes on Banaba. Notably, Grimble was involved in the 1931 Compulsory Land Acquisition. His cadet, Henry Maude, who served as the Native Lands Commissioner on the island from 1931 to 1932, also had a pivotal role in these events. Both Grimble and Maude later gained recognition as notable archaeologists due to their extensive writings and documentation of Banaban history.

Maude acknowledged that much of his work was based on Grimble's original notes collected on Banaba during the pre-war period. He operated under the assumption that much of the island's traditional history had already been lost. He admitted it was 'virtually impossible to get information from Te Aka because of their code of secrecy' (Sigrah & King 2001:32).

What little information he did uncover would be limited and confused with another Banaban clan known as the Mangati, which descended from the Auriaria clan and resided in the Tabwewa district.

This seemingly simple but important mistake would cause further alienation of Banaban identity. It would also cause more confusion and conflict with the Banaban community in later years due to sensitivity over original land boundaries close to the sensitive area where Te Aka sacred cairns once existed (Figure 1.3).

To add to this dilemma, Grimble's early research was taken from interviews with a Banaban woman, Nei Beteua, a direct descendant of Nei Anginimaeao from Tabiang district, and therefore offered a historical perspective based on Gilbertese traditions.

Maude began to realise his mistake while interviewing Banaban landowners and recording the individual land holdings for the first time. It was from this period that he began to report the existence of a pure Banaban identity, 'the Banabans were a unique race, while still referring to only customs and legends that the I-Kiribati introduced to Banaba after the invasion of Nei Anginimaeao' (Sigrah & King 2001:32).

In 1935, Maude and P.D. Macdonald conducted a series of standard anthropometric measurements on 'those Banabans who considered themselves to be of stock unmixed with Gilbertese blood. These numbered 70 in all...', and their results appeared to suggest a difference in certain facial measurements and indices when compared with a control group on Beru. In his 1975 sworn statement to the British

Courts, he would also comment that: 'at all events it was commonly asserted by the late Sir Arthur Grimble and others that a typical Banaban was distinguishable in physical appearance from a Gilbertese, and this I consider to have been the case in a number of the older generation, whose features appeared quite distinctive (Sigrah & King 2001:35).

In this sworn testimony, he would finally admit his original mistake over Banaban identity:

> The view that the Banabans were Gilbertese was indeed uncritically accepted by myself during my early years of residence in the Gilbert and Ellice Colony and it was only after detailed study that it became apparent that, like almost every community the world over, they, in fact, represented a racial mixture, in which the Gilbertese component was a relatively recent overlay on a basically non-Gilbertese stock; and that in any case, the Banabans had never at any time formed a part of the Gilbert Islands, whether geographically, politically or through social cohesion (Sigrah & King 2001: 37).

The recording of incorrect information, however irrelevant it seemed at the time, would have a major and devastating impact on the Banabans in the years following.

13. Early Christian converts on Banaba led by a Missionary Pastor called Solomon (Ellis 1900).

14. The new Banaban *tani Kiritian* (Christian) congregation on Banaba early 1900s (Broadbent Collection).

# 6. The Use of Language to Define Ethnic Identity and Influence of Missionaries

Language has often been used throughout the years to align Banaban identity to the I-Kiribati. This issue has caused argument and debate over the years as the Banabans lament the loss of their original language. This process cannot be entirely blamed on the phosphate mining industry. However, the influx of 'around a thousand recruited Pacific Islands labourers' (Williams & Macdonald 1985:84) who mainly were Gilbertese would also have some impact.

The first introduction of the Gilbertese language began with the arrival of Nei Anginimaeao's group, who had arrived around 200 years earlier. But, this influence was concentrated in the more recent settlements on the island's southern side. The primary catalyst would be the arrival of Captain W. Walkup on 4 August 1885 from the Hawaiian Board of Missions. He quickly 'convinced the Banabans that they could learn much from a mission teacher and the word and stories from the Bible (Baibara) that had been translated into the Kiribati language' (Sigrah & King 2001:195).

Over the next 15 years, half of the Banabans, mainly residing in the southern districts, would embrace the American Congregationalist philosophy, if not always the practices. Meanwhile, Te Aka in the northern district still upheld their old *tani Bakan* (Pagan) ways. Maude would summarise the Banabans 'gradually began building their village churches and schools and learning to read and write with the Gilbertese Bible and other mission-produced literature to help them' (Sigrah & King 2001:197).

This episode would not only formalise the Gilbertese language on the island but also introduce the Banabans to the Western style of education, especially the 'written word'. The missionary influence was so strong that Banabans encouraged them to learn the 'word of God' and adopt the Gilbertese language to receive his message. Maude would also enter into the language debate in his sworn statement to the British Court:

> It is sometimes asserted that the Banabans must be Gilbertese because they speak Gilbertese. Apart from the fact that linguistic affinity is a shaky foundation on which to base racial relationships, this was not

always the case is not only affirmed by the Banabans themselves but was obvious to me when I lived amongst them in 1931-32. During the course of the Land Commission proceedings, which were conducted throughout in the vernacular, I soon became aware that part of the vocabulary and a number of idioms, being used by the witnesses and assessors were not, in fact, Gilbertese at all... though they amounted to a significant quantity, even then, due to the use of the Gilbertese Bible, or Gilbertese as the language of instruction in the mission schools, the influence of the many hundreds of Gilbertese phosphate workers brought to the island under indenture... the Banaban speech had long been swamped by introduced Gilbertese... nevertheless, its former existence is an indication of separate identity while its extinction is attributable to pressures emanating from European contact (Sigrah & King 2001:201).

Maude instructed his court clerk to record these unique Banaban words in a notebook. The original copy of this valuable documented evidence is part of the Maude papers held by the Barr Smith Library, University of Adelaide (Figure 1.8). As mentioned earlier, the other legacy of the lost Banaban language can be found in the words of the distinctive

Te Aka dance *te karanga* (Figure 1.2). Both these crucial records were published by Sigrah & King (2001:201; Appendix 9).

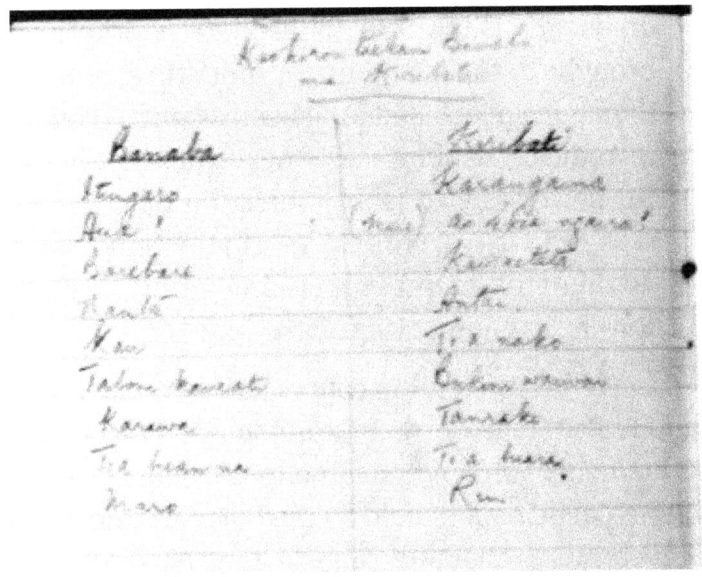

15. Banaban words from Maude's Notebook 1932

# 7. Definition of Banaban Identity and the Value of Land

It is important to record what the Banabans perceive and recognise as their cultural identity.
As previously documented, the Banabans acknowledge three distinct groupings based on the island's history leading to European discovery.

The first grouping is Te Aka, with the recognised head or Godfather as Teimanaia.

The second grouping is based on the first invasion and their Godfather, Auriaria.

The third grouping relates to the arrival of driftaways from the Gilberts and the recognised head, Nei Anginimaeao.

To be considered as a true Banaban or of Banaban blood in today's world, a person has to be related to at least one of these three groupings, and even with inter-marriage many Banabans can still trace their genealogical ancestry back to all three. This status for Banaban identity also highlights the infallible link between land ownership and inherited lineage.

This fact is further endorsed by the Banaban's concept of cultural law known as *te rii ni Banaba* (the backbone of Banaba), used in settling clan disputes, especially concerning land ownership. This process is 'the simple three-point formula given to us by our elders' (Sigrah & King 2001:135) and also forms the fundamental basis of Banaban identity:

1) genealogy,
2) inherited family role,
3) name of hamlet.

In Banaban custom, to earn respect, one has to be acquainted with all aspects of tradition and culture. This knowledge can only be achieved by knowing his or her family's genealogy and the position and inherited duty each individual holds within society. In other words, 'to know one's genealogy is to know one's birthright' (Sigrah & King 2001:56).

The 'claiming of the rights' represents a complicated system of inherited family roles within Banaban society that represents all aspects of daily life, with particular clans recognised as official holders of specific societal duties and rights. 'Many of these duties were introduced into Banaban society as far back as the 16th century through a process of trading for land' (Sigrah & King 2001:133).

The naming of your hamlet represents the clan's inherited land ownership. These three points are of critical importance as each one interlocks with the other, proving indigenous Banaban identity and the overwhelming link to land.

The Banaban system of cultural law, '*te rii ni Banaba,*' is still practised today.

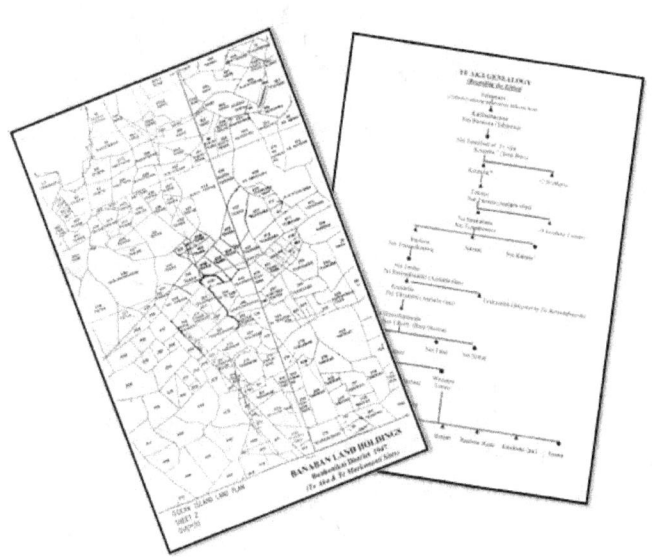

16. Cultural Law, *Te Rii ni Banaba*: Know your genealogy, inherited family role, and name of your hamlet.

17, Phosphate mining nearing Te Aka village site in 1965 (Lampert Collection).

# 8. Te Aka Discovery

The existence of the Te Aka was virtually unknown outside of the Banaban community. The clan's strict code of secrecy and powers of sorcery are well known and respected among the Banabans. These traits also aided in keeping their existence obscure. While many of the new European arrivals started to interact with the local inhabitants, especially men like Ellis, Mahaffy, Grimble and Maude, who began to record Banaban folklore and sociology, the Te Aka shied away from any foreign contact.

This is evidenced by the first invasion of Banaba by Auriaria when Te Aka fought the invaders and upheld land boundaries and the whole northern side of the island over the centuries that followed right up to the mining of their land.

Even with the arrival of missionaries, many of the Te Aka refused to convert to Christianity. They upheld their traditional pagan beliefs, evoking powers from their ancestral skulls and practising their rituals based on sun worship. The missionary influence over half of the island's inhabitants from

1885 onwards would aid in creating a cultural divide where the Christians would begin learning new concepts based on Western ways and the Land of Matang (the place where the fair-skinned men dwelled), especially in education.

The gap between the old and new ways would emerge with the formal introduction of Gilbertese language through the Bible and Banabans being sent abroad to missionary school. By the time of Ellis' arrival in 1900, his Christian values and more gentlemanly ways proved a welcomed relief from the earlier beachcombers and driftaways the Banabans had experienced in the past.

Ellis quickly aligned himself with his fellow Christians and used the local missionaries to his advantage, especially those with a grasp of English. This development would further alienate Te Aka and only build to the mystery and fear surrounding them.

No mention of them would appear in any historical writing. In Maude's 1932 article on Banaban Social Organisation, he described, 'according to local myth the original inhabitants of Banaba were Melanesian in type'. His information was confusing, and no mention of the Te Aka appears, but snippets of valuable insight can be found:

> A portion of this host, whose ancestor was Auriaria, landed on Banaban and succeeded in overcoming the inhabitants, 'casting

them into the sea,' though they had a wholesome fear of their sorcery... However, it would appear from local tradition that not all of the black folk were killed, for a remnant appears to have been driven to the central plateau of the island...' (Maude & Maude 1932: 264)

Unfortunately, he would mistakenly identify the Te Aka as the Mangati people and the 'people of Tairua [Taaira]' when no such place exists and no family or hamlet are known by this name. 'The word Taaira or Tairua as the Banabans spell it means 'foreigner', and the word Banabans associate with as the Battle of Tairua,'. (Sigrah & King 2001:143).

Once again, it must be remembered that the Banabans would only refer to Te Aka and their settlement on the island as te Aonoanne, 'that place!', because of the curse they were convinced would befall them at the mere mention of the name. Maude (1997) would admit that 'while he was researching traditional Banaban history, it was virtually impossible to get information from Te Aka because of their code of secrecy' (Sigrah & King 2001:32).

The physical and scientific evidence of the existence of Te Aka and their old sacred village site would not be discovered until the Company began preliminary preparations to mine an area on the central plateau near the old wireless station in 1965. Even with the removal of the Banabans from the island in 1943 by the Japanese and their subsequent resettlement on Rabi over 3,200 kilometres away in the Fiji Group, the fear and mystery surrounding this area remained.

In 1964, BPC employees discovered an old village site in the interior while they were preparing the area for mining. This initially involved clearing overlying vegetation and removing the land surface, which threatened to destroy the site. Mining was postponed to the immediate area, and the Company informed the Bishop Museum in Honolulu and the Australian National University in Canberra of the discovery.

A joint archaeological investigation was conducted by Dr Ronald Lampert with the assistance of Professor John Golson of ANU's Department of Anthropology and Dr K.P. Emroy from Bishop University. Lampert spent three weeks excavating the site with a full-time labour force of two I-Kiribati and one Tuvaluan, Mrs Lorraine Thwaites, and volunteers among the BPC's European staff (Sigrah & King 2001:266).

Lampert verified and confirmed the site as that of the old Te Aka site and noted the different sources of identification. He also located an old BPC map dated 1907 that showed six 'native houses' that had survived at the location.

Following the re-discovery of the site, the BPC had mapped the floor plans of the buildings in detail, and with the aid of this map and his own examination, Lampert was able to identify the existence of at least a dozen buildings that had been represented at the site over time. One of the building sites was identified as a *maneaba* (meeting house), part of it having already been accidentally bulldozed before his arrival.

The most valuable find to be uncovered were the skeletal remains of two individuals found in the earth-filled extension of the *maneaba,* and a third burial site was located in one of the other building sites. The first remains consisted of a skull only, while the second burial site contained an incomplete skeleton with the skull and long bones of the legs completely missing. These bones were in poor condition, while the third remains were in good condition and missing the skull.

He would also discover other artifacts, including various types of adzes used as cutting edges, shell-type ornaments, partly finished stalactite fishing hooks and weights used for frigate bird snaring. Lamperts' findings would conclude that Te Aka village had been occupied until fairly recently, and wood samples were analysed by Mr Polach from the C-14 Dating Laboratory at ANU to be less than 200 years old. Later, carbon dating tests on charcoal taken from one of the cooking pits would date the relevant sample back to 300 to 400 years (Sigrah & King 2001:281).

Lampert also commented that the finding of the remains would endorse the practice whereby relatives of the deceased would often retain the skull and certain other bones to make tools such as fish hooks and shuttles used for thatch roofing. A femur bone from the third burial site was sent to G.C. Schofield from the Department of Anatomy at Monash University for extensive examination. He found that the bone was a right-sided femur of an adult female and was obviously not Polynesian (Sigrah & King 2001: 35,282; Lampert 1968:17)

Once Lampert had removed the remains and artefacts for safe storage and assessment back at ANU, the mining would resume, and the site would be completely destroyed. It would not be until 1997 that Lampert would discover the significance of the site and its value to the Banaban people.

He was also shocked to learn that the plans to mine the site had been cancelled not long after he had finished his investigations. The sudden unexplained death of an overseer involved in mining the area had finally brought the mining to a halt.

Now, more than 44 years since the cessation of mining on Banaba, Te Aka remains unmined, all except for the original surface clearing that was conducted before Lampert's arrival. Today, the site is completely encircled by a 'fortress' of towering limestone pinnacles, making access virtually impossible. While the superstitions regarding Te Aka live on, this sacred place has been again enveloped and shrouded in mystery. The skeletal remains and artifacts kept at ANU were finally returned to the Banaban community on Rabi in 1998.

18. Archeological dig conducted at the old Te Aka village site by Dr Ronald Lampert 1966 (Lampert Collection).

# 9. Banaban assimilation – fact or fiction

The question of Banaban identity was never an issue leading up to World War Two. However, once the Banabans were removed from the island in 1943 by the invading Japanese forces and subsequently relocated to Rabi, Fiji, in 1945, the situation of the Banabans became very tenuous.

From the post-war period onwards, as mining on the island moved back into full production, the island's European staff had virtually no idea or understanding of the Banabans. With the island's labour staff comprised of thousands of Gilbertese (I-Kiribati) and Ellice (Tuvaluan) islanders, the legitimacy of Banaba's indigenous population became obscure.

It was during this time that the idea of Banaban assimilation with Kiribati seemed to intensify. With European Company staff having no direct contact with the Banabans and the influx of such a large number of Kiribati labourers dominating the island's workforce, the notation of Banabans being 'troublemakers' began to grow. This catch cry had originally been generated from the Company management instructing their staff 'not to mix with these Banaban troublemakers' (Lennon 1992), and grew over the years, becoming the status quo with Banabans relocated over 3,200 kilometres away in Rabi, Fiji.

Until the mid-1970s, the presence of one lone Banaban representative and his family living on the island was the only contact the Banabans and the people living and working on the island would have. This important but difficult role would also endorse the Company's claims, especially over the years as the Banabans became more dissenting and began legal action against the Company.

In January 1974, the Banabans unsuccessfully petitioned the British Government 'calling for the separation of Ocean Island from the Gilbert and Ellice Island Colony and the recognition of Ocean Island's independence' (Sigrah & King 2001:18).

When a Banaban contingent of over 100 young Banabans arrived on the island in 1977 and again in 1979 to stake their claim to the homeland while their legal proceedings were underway in the British Courts, the situation was tense, with Banabans forced to live in a makeshift camp down on the beach behind their old village site of Uma. The Banaban aims were to try and stop mining while their court case was underway, and their protests had turned violent, resulting in the death of one of their young men.

The court case against the British Government and the British Phosphate Commission (BPC) finally ended in 1979, becoming known as one of the most protracted civil court cases in UK history. It was during this tumultuous period that the argument of Banaban-Kiribati assimilation came to the fore.

Another contributing factor to the argument would go back to the removal of the Banabans from their homeland by the Japanese occupation force in 1943 and their dispersal to Japanese camps in Kosrae, Nauru and Tarawa.

By the end of the war in 1945, when the Banabans were gathered together on Tarawa with the aim of relocating them to Fiji, from the 1,003 war survivors brought together, 703 were listed as being Banabans, while 300 were I-Kiribati. This I-Kiribati influx had grown over the war period from their forced relocation to other Pacific islands, resulting in new relationships and intermarriages. This group would form the nucleus of the new Banaban settlement, arriving on Rabi 15 Dec 1945.

Over the years of mining, it is correct that there were a number of inter-marriages between the islanders, including the Ellis (Tuvalu) and Fiji contingents, with some of the imported labour staff being adopted into Banaban families. Still, traditional Banaban customs, especially regarding marriage, sports, dances, claiming of the rights (inherited roles within the community, based on cultural law of '*te rii ni Banaba*'), adoption, and the elders' position within the *maneaba* were all maintained.

The Banaban elders were diligent in upholding their cultural and ethnic identity even after the relocation to Rabi, with certain dances and sports of Kiribati origins banned from official gatherings to ensure that these important cultural practices were respected and preserved for future generations (Sigrah & King 2001:162-164).

19. First Banaban generation born on Rabi, Fiji after 1945.

## 10. Banabans Today Living Under Two Governments – Fiji and Kiribati

Today, the Banabans find themselves living under two different Pacific Nations. This process further complicates their quest to uphold cultural identity while observing the laws and traditions of living in a foreign land. While Pacific islanders uphold great respect for their Island brothers, the customs and traditions that are essential in everyday life, and more importantly, the survival of cultural identity in a rapidly changing world, are very much under threat.

In the past, especially following their resettlement on Rabi, Banaban elders made every effort to safeguard and preserve Banaban identity for future generations. Today, with many of the elders having passed away and a new generation facing significant challenges, the Banabans are at greater risk than ever of being fully assimilated into mainstream Kiribati and Fijian societies.

20. Banaban Elders on Rabi, 1995 (S. King Collection).

The mining company operated under the assumption that assimilation would be the most effective way to facilitate their extraction of resources from Banaba. History has shown that past colonial officials who tried to protect the Banabans' interests in the early mining days would be sent packing.

The idea of moving the Banabans to another island was first raised back in 1914 (Maude1946:10), and documentation from the Prime Minister of Australia to the Dominions Office in 1927 would also support these plans (Sigrah & King 2001: 239,323).

The Japanese invasion of Banaba would provide the perfect solution to removing Banabans permanently from their homeland. Today, the Banaban community on the homeland currently numbers around 250 to 300 who live amongst the crumbling asbestos-ridden wreckage and decaying buildings left by the mining company.

Banaba now comes under the laws and jurisdiction of the Kiribati Constitution with the interpretation of a 'Banaban' or 'Banabans' defined as 'the former indigenous inhabitants of Banaba and such other persons one of whose ancestors was born in Kiribati before 1900 as may now or hereafter be accepted as members of the Banaban community in accordance with custom' (See Chapter IX, section 125). They have two Banaban representatives in the Kiribati Assembly, one representing Banaba and the other representing Rabi.

Between the Banabans arrival on Rabi in 1945 and 1995, the Banaban community on Rabi grew from 1,003 to over 5,000. The Banaban Settlement Ordinance of 1945 (Cap.104) set up the framework for the administration of Rabi Island and provided for Rabi's administration through a separate island council. However, resettled Banabans were otherwise subject to Fiji law.

Banabans were quoted as 'enjoying a unique position in Fiji' by the Committee that conducted the Inquiry into Rabi Island Council Affairs in April 1994. Their report also stated that:

> The Banabans of Rabi are citizens of Fiji with full voting and electoral rights, yet they also have a representative in the Kiribati Assembly representing the Banaban community in Fiji. They have the right to free entry and residence on both Banaban and Rabi. They have been given wide powers to govern themselves on Rabi, they may set their own taxes and rates, they have the sole right to administer their land, they may establish their own police force. In many respects they have greater autonomy than the Rotumans.

Yet, with all these provisions in place, why are the Banabans today under such threat? In May 2003 a report commissioned by the Commission on Human Rights regarding the Minority Rights in Fiji and the Solomon Island painted an alarming picture:

> Aid dependency and poor financial management have led to deteriorating living standards for the Banaban community of

Rabi. After the misappropriation of funds in the 1980s and a failure to meet debts in 1992, the Rabi Island Council was briefly dissolved by the Fiji government. Banabans remain one of Fiji's most disadvantaged and politically marginalised communities. Affirmative action programmes for Indigenous Fiji and Rotuman communities in the aftermath of the 1987 and 2000 coups have not been targeted at Banaban people.

The report would go on to state that the 'settlers from their once phosphate-rich island of Banaba find themselves trapped in a position of social deprivation, and exclusion from mainstream political processes'.

Past Faces of Banaban Identity

The Faces of Banaban Identity Today...

# 11. Conclusion

To preserve Banaban ethnic identity, three key factors must be addressed: education, unity, and autonomy. For centuries, the traditional Banaban teachings emphasised that 'secrecy is the fortification of identity,' a principle that safeguarded Banaban knowledge and values across generations.

As Banabans face new challenges and the threat of assimilation into Fijian and Kiribati societies, it is more important than ever to embrace and preserve the cultural practices unique to Banaba. Keeping Banaban history alive in the present is crucial so that when future generations return to their homeland and touch the soil, it will remind them of who they are and where they truly belong.

To strengthen Banaban claims for autonomy that would provide a voice in the areas of formal recognition, education policies and legal freedoms and rights in today's world, the Banabans first have to understand the basic principles needed to achieve this goal. While autonomy is generally un To strengthen Banaban claims for autonomy—

particularly in areas such as formal recognition, education policies, and legal rights—the Banabans must first grasp the fundamental principles required to achieve this goal. Autonomy, generally understood as the ability to live according to one's own values and free from external manipulation, hinges on two key components essential for self-governance.

Before one can govern oneself, one must first be able to act competently based on desires and values that are truly one's own. For the Banabans to build a strong future, the strength must come from within, driven by a united movement. This movement must be grounded in human kindness, spiritual unity, and a deep respect for the dignity of every individual—principles that can achieve far more than any form of oppression, persecution, or denial of freedom ever could.

The history of the Banabans is one of colonisation, in which a colonising culture was actively promoted to replace their indigenous culture. The term 'folklore' is not an acceptable term to the Banabans. Their culture is not 'folklore' but the sacred law intertwined with a traditional way of life – the laws that set the legal, moral, and cultural values of Banaban traditional society.

They are Banaban cultural identity.

# References

*Autonomy in Moral and Political Philosophy.* Stanford Encyclopedia of Philosophy.

Aiden, C., Ratuvuki, L., Teai, T. *Report of the Committee of Inquiry into the Rabi Island Council Affairs.* Government Buildings, Suva. Fiji. 8 April 1994.

Ellice, A.F. *Ocean Island and Nauru.* Sydney: Angus & Robertson Ltd, 1936.

Fraenkel, John. *Minority Right in Fiji and The Solomon Island: Reinforcing Constitutional Protections, Establishing Land Rights and Overcoming Poverty.* University of the South Pacific. 12-16 May 2003

Grimble, A. *From Birth to Death in the Gilbert Islands.* Journal of the Royal Anthropological Institute, 1921.

Kiribati Legislation - *The Constitution of Kiribati.* Pacific Law Materials.

Lampert, R.J. *Anthropological Investigation of Te Aka Village, Ocean Island: Preliminary Report.*

Canberra, Department of Anthropology, Australian National University, 1965.

Lampert, R.J. *An Anthropological Investigation of Ocean Island, Central Pacific. Archaeology and Physical Anthropology in Oceania*, Vol. 111, No.1. April, 1968

Lennon, Edna. Former wife of BPC employee 1950-1965. Interview conducted by S.King, 1992.

Mahaffy, Arthur. *Ocean Island.* Blackwood's Magazine, November, 1910.

Maude, Harry and Honor. Recorded Interview conducted by K. Sigrah and S. King, Canberra. 1997.

Maude, H.E. *Memorandum on The Future of the Banaban Population of Ocean Island; With Special Relations to their Lands and Funds.* Chief Lands Commissioner, Gilbert and Ellice Islands Colony, 1946.

Maude, H.C. and H.E. *The Book of Banaba.* IPS, University of South Pacific Fiji, 1995. Maude, H.C. and H.E. *The Social Organisation of Banaba or Ocean Island of Banaba or Ocean Island, Central Pacific,* Journal of the Polynesian Society 41, 1932.

Sigrah, Raobeia Ken and King, Stacey M. *Te Rii ni Banaba.* IPS, University of South Pacific Fiji, 2001.(2$^{nd}$ edition: Banaban Vision Publication 2019).

Sivia, Tora. Report on the Pacific Regional Seminar. Director of Culture and Heritage, Ministry of Culture and Heritage, Fiji Island. 11-13 February, 1999.

Walkup, Alfred. *Report of the First Voyage of the Missionary Barkantine 'Morning Star' to Micronesia, 1885.* Boston, American Board of Commissioners for Foreign Missions. 1885

Watson, Lilla. Welcome: Amnesty International Conference: Brisbane, 4 Sept 2004

Webster, John. n.d. *The Last Cruise of the Wanderer.* Sydney, F. Cunninghame. [1851]

Williams, Maslyn and Macdonald, Barrie. *The Phosphateers.* Melbourne University Press 1985.

21. The authors returning the female remains recovered from the Te Aka dig by Lampert in 1960s to the Te Aka Clan residing on Rabi Island, 2000.

# About the Authors

RAOBEIA KEN SIGRAH
1956 – 2021

The late Raobeia Ken Sigrah was born on 18 January 1956 on Rabi, Fiji. He identified as a Banaban but held a Fiji passport and later resided in Australia. Known as Ken to his friends, he began his education at the age of seven at Buakonikai Primary

School in 1962 and continued at Banaban Primary School until 1967. After passing his Intermediate exams, he attended Niusawa Methodist High School, a Fijian school on nearby Taveuni. In 1980, he studied English for a year at Fulton College in Fiji.

In 1972, Ken was employed as a clerk for the Rabi Council of Leaders in the Public Works Department. Around this time, he joined the Banaban Dancing Group, which represented the Council culturally and performed abroad. That same year, Ken travelled with the group at the invitation of Australian authorities to perform at the opening ceremonies of the Sydney Opera House, facilitated by the Fiji Arts Theatre. The group also performed in Brisbane during the tour. In 1974, Ken toured Nauru, Banaba, and Tarawa with the dancing group while still working as a clerk for the Rabi Council. In 1975, he attended the South Pacific Festival of Arts in Rotorua, New Zealand. After this trip, he left the dancing group but continued working for the Rabi Council.

In 1979, Ken joined a group of young Banaban men and elders on a significant trip to Banaba just before mining operations ceased. After nine months on Banaba, he returned to Rabi. By 1982, he was employed by the Fiji government as a clerk and storeman, a position he held for six years until he resigned in 1989. He was then re-employed by the Rabi Council as a Labour Officer and Inspector. He resigned again from the Council in 1990 and returned to a traditional Banaban lifestyle.

Ken studied Banaban culture and customs under the guidance of Banaban elders. He began these studies at the age of 14, as part of his responsibilities as a male clan member, preparing to serve as a clan spokesman in meetings concerning Banaban culture, customs, and genealogies. Ken witnessed the challenges his people faced and represented individual clans in general meetings, exchanging ideas with Banaban elders. His first experience as a clan spokesman was in 1987, followed by further roles in 1994, 1995, and 1996.

In 1997, Ken asked Stacey King to assist him in writing a history of Banaba. His aim was to promote Banaban history, culture, and customs, though he had previously struggled to find a sponsor for editing and publishing the work. With many elders having passed away and others in their later years, he hoped to publish this material, gathered over many years, for the benefit of the younger Banaban generation, who are now growing up in a different environment, to help them preserve their culture, heritage, and identity as Banabans.

STACEY M. KING

Stacey M. King is a historian, author, entrepreneur, and philanthropist. She has been an advocate for the indigenous Banaban people for many decades. In 1989, she began researching her family's history for a historical novel based on their lives titled – *Nakaa's Awakening: Land of Matang* (Book One; 2000).

In 1997, she formed a personal and collaborative partnership with the late Ken Raobeia Sigrah, a Banaban Clan historian and spokesperson. Their first published work, *Te Rii Ni Banaba - backbone of*

*Banaba* (2001; 2019), is a history book written from an indigenous perspective and endorsed by Banaban Clan elders.

With the establishment of Banaban Vision Publications, Stacey is converting much of their writings and research findings into digital publications. Since the passing of her beloved partner, Raobeia Ken Sigrah, she has been determined to continue his legacy in preserving Banaban history for future generations.

22. The authors meeting with Dr Lampert at ANU, Canberra 1997 to arrange the return of artefacts recovered from Te Aka dig in 1960s. (S. King Collection 1997).

# Other Titles By The Authors

### Banaban History Non-Fiction Book
*Te Rii ni Banaba backbone of Banaba.* First Edition: IPS, Suva, Fiji. 2001, Second edition, Banaban Vision Publications, Gold Coast, Australia 2019.
*Australia Banaba Relations: the Price of Shaping a Nation.* Banaban Vision, Gold Coast, March 2023.
*Legacy of a Miner's daughter: the impact on the Banabans after phosphate mining.* Banaban Vision Publications, Gold Coast, Australia 2023.

### History Non-Fiction Book – Chapter in Book
*The Banaba-Ocean Island chronicles: private collections, indigenous record-keeping, fact and fiction*. Chapter 17, *Hunting the Collectors*. Cambridge Scholars, UK.

### Historical Fiction
*Nakaa's Awakening, Land of Matang.* Banaban Vision Publications, Gold Coast, Australia, 2020

(Book 1; 4-book series. Blend of history, biography and fictional reconstruction)

## Articles and Presentations

*Australia Banaba Relations: the price of shaping a nation is now a call for recognition.* Adapted from Conference Paper: The Pacific in Australia 2006.
This paper was presented at The Pacific in Australia - Australia in the Pacific conference QUT, Carseldine campus, Brisbane, Australia 24 to 27 January 2006 - The Pacific and Australia - Australia in the Pacific; Humanities research - History.

*Banaba-Ocean Island Chronicles: Private collections and indigenous record-keeping proving fact from fiction.* Conference Paper: The Pacific in Australia 2006. This paper was presented at The Pacific in Australia - Australia in the Pacific conference QUT, Carseldine campus, Brisbane, Australia 24 to 27 January 2006 - The Pacific and Australia - Australia in the Pacific; Humanities research - History.

*Cultural Identity of Banabans*
Adapted from a Conference Paper: ISLANDS of the WORLD VIII Taiwan. This paper was presented and published at ISLANDS of the WORLD VIII International Conference "Changing Islands – Changing Worlds" 1-7 November 2004, Kinmen Island (Quemoy), Taiwan.

*Legacy of a Miners Daughter and Assessment of the Social Changes of the Banabans after Phosphate Mining on Banaba*

Adapted from a Conference Paper: ISLANDS of the WORLD VIII Taiwan. This paper was presented and published at ISLANDS of the WORLD VIII International Conference "Changing Islands – Changing Worlds"1-7 November 2004, Kinmen Island (Quemoy), Taiwan.

*Essentially Being Banaban in Today's World: The Role of Banaban Law, Te Rii Ni Banaba (Backbone of Banaba) in a Changing World*.

Conference Paper: ISLANDS of the WORLD VIII Taiwan. This paper was presented and published at ISLANDS of the WORLD VIII International Conference "Changing Islands – Changing Worlds"1-7 November 2004, Kinmen Island (Quemoy), Taiwan.

## Banaban Social Media sites by Authors

Abara Banaba–Come Meet the Banabans: banaban.com
Banaban Vision: banabanvision.com
Banaban Voice Facebook:
facebook.com/groups/banabanvoice/
Banaban Vision Blog: banabanvoice.ning.com/
Banaban Vision: banabanvision.com
Banaban Media: vocalmedia.com

## Connect:

Banaban Vision Publications
PO Box 1116 Paradise Point Qld 4216 Australia
Stacey M. King – Author's Page: staceymking.com

Email: admin@banaban.com
Te Rii Ni Banaba -Facebook group:
https://www.facebook.com/groups/296299534653304/
Linkedin: Ken Sigrah:
https://www.linkedin.com/in/ken-sigrah-821b5975/
Linkedin: Stacey King:
https://www.linkedin.com/in/stacey-king-4ba68a76/

www.ingramcontent.com/pod-product-compliance
Lightning Source LLC
Chambersburg PA
CBHW071837290426
44109CB00017B/1846